it's a

Good Day

to have a

Good Day

AN

ASK & IT IS

WRITTEN

AFFIRMATION

BOOK

DONNA KOZIK

Donna Kozik
San Diego, Calif.
www.AskAndItIsWritten.com

Limits of Liability
The author and publisher shall not be liable for your misuse of this material. This book is strictly for informational and educational purposes.

Disclaimer
The purpose of this book is to educate and entertain. The author and/or publisher do not guarantee that anyone following these techniques, suggestions, tips, ideas, or strategies will become successful. The author and/or publisher shall have neither liability nor responsibility to anyone with respect to any loss or damage caused, or alleged to be caused, directly or indirectly by the information contained in this book.

Paperback: 979-8-9990420-0-2

it's a
Good Day
to have a
Good Day

AN

ASK & IT IS

WRITTEN

AFFIRMATION

BOOK

DONNA KOZIK

GET YOUR FREE GIFT

Pick up affirmations, writing prompts and more at the official "Ask & It Is Written" website to start your day on a positive note!

Go to www.AskAndItIsWritten.com to get your free gift!

Your Invitation to Join the Ask & It Is Written Community

At Ask & It Is Written, we believe in the profound power of words—the words we read, write, speak, and share. Founded on principles of connection, inspiration, and spiritual alignment, we're dedicated to nurturing a vibrant community where your voice matters.

Through our journals, affirmation books, and community circles, we help you discover and develop your inner leader—guiding you to clarity, confidence, and creativity. Here, writing is not just self-expression; it's an act of creation, transformation, and community-building.

Meanwhile, the Ask & It Is Written publishing imprint supports authors who seek to uplift, inspire, and transform readers through thoughtfully crafted books and journals. Each publication under this imprint is intentionally designed to encourage spiritual growth and personal empowerment.

We invite you to become part of a supportive network of like-minded individuals committed to personal growth, spiritual depth, and joyful leadership. Whether you're new to writing or a seasoned author, you'll find inspiration and camaraderie at *Ask & It Is Written*.

Welcome to the community.

Let's write the next beautiful chapter together.

For more, visit:
www.AskAndItIsWritten.com.

ACKNOWLEDGMENTS

"It's a Good Day to Have a Good Day" is inspired by the uplifting phrase Tim Trausch repeated each morning: "Today is a good day to have a good day." After his ALS diagnosis, Tim chose to meet each day with courage and a smile—his mantra became a gentle but powerful reminder to find good in the moment, no matter the circumstances. His spirit and words stay with me, and I'm honored to carry them forward here. I also gratefully acknowledge country music legend Bill Anderson, whose song of a similar name adds another layer of heart and harmony to this message of hope.

To my incredible community of clients and writers—you provide the spark for so many of my ideas and the talent to see them brought to life. Working with you is a joy and an inspiration. Your stories, your goals, and your willingness to show up for your dreams continually remind me why I do this work. Thank you for trusting me to walk alongside you.

On a personal note, and with heartfelt gratitude, I want to thank my sister, Teresa A. Castleman, and my brother-in-law, Brad Castleman, for always being there to cheer me on. Your love, encouragement, and belief in me mean more than I can ever say. A big thank you as well to Publishing Manager Elijah Toten—your talent, dedication, and behind-the-scenes support keep everything running smoothly, and your enthusiasm is a gift that keeps everyone's spirits high.

Thank you to Ruth Strebe for being a

fabulous sounding board and Tara Myers for keeping the faith.

I'm also grateful to my housemates, Lowell Norman and Tyler Norman, for the many dinners shared and the rich, thoughtful conversations that always seem to spark something new. Your presence makes life fuller—and tastier.

DEDICATION

For the seekers of light in ordinary days, the brave ones who rise again and again, and the quiet hearts choosing joy on purpose.

This book is for you.

ABOUT THE AUTHOR

Donna Kozik is the founder of Ask & It Is Written, a spiritually rooted publishing imprint, community and movement that helps people turn powerful questions into trans-formational books, journals, and other offerings. A USA Today & Wall Street Journal bestselling author, Donna has made it her mission to get people published—and to do it with purpose and ease.

For nearly two decades, she's led the popular Write a Book in a Weekend® program and now offers Done for You Publishing services for coaches, consultants, and mission-driven entrepreneurs who want to make a meaningful impact with their message. Her signature approach blends clarity, confidence, and creativity—anchored in the belief that words (and questions) can change lives.

Donna grew up on a 200-acre dairy farm outside of Erie, Pennsylvania, and now lives near the beaches and freeways of San Diego, California. The Pacific Northwest, especially Astoria, Oregon, is one of her favorite places to visit.

She invites you to join the Ask & It Is Written movement—and start writing the next beautiful chapter of your life and business.

Get her free Book Planner at www.FreeBookPlanner.com

Discover more about the publishing imprint at www.AskAndItIsWritten.com

WELCOME

You picked up this book for a reason. Maybe it was the title—bright, simple, and true. Maybe you were looking for something to lift your spirits, anchor your morning, or remind you that today is, in fact, a fresh start. However you arrived here, I'm glad you did.

This book is a companion, a pocket of sunshine, a quiet nudge when you need it most. It's not about being perfect or positive all the time—it's about choosing to show up with a little more hope, a little more heart, and a whole lot of grace.

Inside, you'll find affirmations to speak life into your day, and simple practices to help you stay grounded, grateful, and open to joy. These aren't complicated rituals or rigid routines. They're light touches of intention—playful and spiritual ways to remember who you are and what really matters.

You don't have to read this book in order. You don't have to do every practice. Just flip to a page, take what resonates, and leave the rest. Let your heart lead. Let your soul stretch. Let your smile shine bright.

Because no matter what yesterday looked like, or what tomorrow holds, today is still a good day to have a good day.

Welcome in.

Let's begin.

How to Use This Book

There's no wrong way to have a good day—just like there's no wrong way to use this book. This is your space. Your reset button. Your permission slip. Your daily spark.

You can begin at the beginning or flip to any page that calls to you. Use it like a morning ritual, a midday pick-me-up, or an end-of-day reflection. Keep it by your bedside, toss it in your bag, or place it where you'll see it when you need a dose of joy or peace.

Here are a few ideas to try:
- **Start your day with an affirmation.** Repeat in your head while brushing your teeth or say it out loud between sips of coffee. Let it set the tone for your day.
- **Choose a theme for the week.** Spend time with one section—like Morning Mindset or Creative Spark—and

weave that energy into your days.

- **Use the Good Day Practices as spiritual play.** Try one a day, or pick one when you need a moment of magic, grounding, or reconnection.
- **Say it, write it, post it.** Turn your favorite affirmation into a sticky note on your mirror or a journal prompt for deeper reflection.
- **Share it.** Read an affirmation to a friend. Leave a note on someone's desk. Use this book to ripple kindness outward and forward.

There's no checklist. No right order. Just invitations to return to yourself again and again—with love, curiosity, and intention.

Let this book be what you need it to be: a nudge, a balm, a reminder, a celebration.

You don't have to fix the whole day. Just meet it with an open heart. And remember: *It's a good day to have a good day.*

Contents

Morning Mindset

I rise with joy
and curiosity.

Today is already filled
with possibilities.

I am ready to receive
all the goodness
this day holds.

I wake with peace
in my heart and
purpose in my step.

—◆—

The morning greets
me with open arms.

—◆—

I begin today with love
in my thoughts and
gratitude in my bones.

Each breath I take
is a fresh start.

＊

I am the light I've
been waiting for.

＊

The world is
brighter because
I am in it today.

I move into this day
with ease and delight.

❖

My presence is
powerful from the
very first moment.

❖

This day was
made for me.

I bring light to every
room I enter.

I choose faith over
fear this morning.

I welcome the flow
of good things
toward me.

**My joy begins
before coffee.**

❦

**I am fully alive
and fully available
to miracles.**

❦

**The sunrise reminds
me of what's possible.**

I align with peace
before I align with
my schedule.

———◆———

I start slow and
shine bright.

———◆———

My energy sets the
tone for the day.

I awaken my spirit
and stretch into hope.

⌐———◆———⌐

I am grateful for this
gift of a new day.

⌐———◆———⌐

I am divinely guided
from the moment

⌐———◆———⌐

I open my eyes. Today
is already blessed.

Good Day Practices for a
MORNING MINDSET

- Wake up and say, *"Thank you, today."*

- Stretch your arms to the sky like you're greeting the sun.

- Open a window and take three deep breaths of fresh air.

- Make your bed with love, not obligation.

- Place your feet on the floor and say, *"I am grounded. I am guided."*

- Set an intention in the shower: *"Let this water wash off yesterday."*

- Stir love into your morning drink—literally imagine the joy in the cup.

- Smile at yourself in the mirror, even if it feels silly. Especially if it does.

- Say a quick blessing over your calendar or to-do list.

- Play your favorite feel-good song before checking your phone.

- Visualize one good thing happening today.

- Whisper a prayer for strength and joy before you walk out the door.

- Say yes to yourself before you say yes to the world.

- Light incense or diffuse essential oils and say, *"I am creating sacred space."*

- Say: *"This day is a gift, and I get to decide how to open it."*

Midday Reset

I pause and come
home to myself.

⟡

This moment is a
sacred restart.

⟡

I am allowed to
begin again.

I breathe deeply
and soften my
grip on the day.

❦

I am calm, centered,
and renewed.

❦

Peace is only one
breath away.

I give myself
permission to
slow down.

———◆———

I step back into
grace and ease.

———◆———

My stillness holds
great power.

I am present, not
pressured.

❦

In this moment,
everything is enough.

❦

I reset my energy and
release all tension.

I trust the rhythm
of my day.

＊

I receive this pause
as a blessing.

＊

My inner peace resets
the outer pace.

**I carry divine calm
into the second
half of my day.**

———◆———

**I inhale clarity and
exhale stress.**

———◆———

**I align with flow,
not force.**

Every breath invites
me back to balance.

❖

I welcome rest as part
of my productivity.

❖

I am worthy of
quiet moments.

❖

I let go of what's
not mine to carry.

I breathe in God's
grace, I breathe
out all doubt.

My midday moment
recharges my spirit.

I choose softness
over struggle.

Good Day Practices for a
MIDDAY RESET

- Take a one-minute pause with your hand on your belly and breathe.

- Look away from screens and focus on something alive—tree, bird, flower.

- Say this aloud: *"I am allowed to begin again, right now."*

- Step outside and feel the sun or wind on your face.

- Set a timer and do absolutely nothing for two minutes.

- Shake out your arms like you're shaking off stress.

- Drink water like it's holy—feel it cleanse you.

- Close your eyes and imagine light

pouring down on you.

- Delete one thing from your list and say, *"Less is good today."*

- Eat something with full attention and gratitude.

- Dance in your kitchen for 30 seconds.

- Say: *"I trust myself to handle what comes next."*

- Text a friend and tell them something good about their spirit.

- Find something that smells good and inhale it slowly.

- Lay flat on the ground and let it support you.

Self-Love & Worthiness

I am already enough.

⸺⸺◈⸺⸺

I treat myself with
tenderness and truth.

⸺⸺◈⸺⸺

I am worthy of all the
love I give so freely.

My value is not
up for debate.

❦

I honor myself by
being kind to myself.

❦

I am a masterpiece
in motion.

I deserve care,
compassion, and joy.

— ◆ —

I belong here
exactly as I am.

— ◆ —

I radiate from within.

I accept all of me—
flaws, fears, and fire.

⸻◆⸻

I give myself the grace
I give to others.

⸻◆⸻

My love for myself
is my foundation.

I am allowed to take
up space and time.

⟡

I cherish my heart, my
voice, and my spirit.

⟡

I am lovable at every
stage of becoming.

I am not too much.
I am just right.

———◆———

I release comparison
and embrace my
own path.

———◆———

I listen to the
wisdom within me.

I am not broken.
I am becoming.

My soul shines
brighter when I love
myself deeply.

I don't need fixing. I
need remembering.

I am a divine
expression of love.

⬥

I celebrate who I am,
not just who I will be.

⬥

I walk in worthiness.

⬥

I am the love I've
been looking for.

Good Day Practices for
SELF-LOVE & WORTHINESS

- Say "I love you" to yourself in the mirror.

- Hug yourself. Seriously. Wrap your arms around your body.

- Forgive yourself for something tiny—and smile when you do.

- Write your name and decorate it like it's precious art.

- Look at an old photo and send that version of you love.

- Touch your face gently and say, *"You are worthy of care."*

- Take one thing off your plate and say, *"I choose ease."*

- Compliment yourself out loud for something no one else sees.

- Say: *"I am allowed to want what I want."*

- Imagine your highest self giving you a pep talk.

- Wrap up in a blanket and call it a blessing cloak.

- Turn off notifications for one hour—your peace matters.

- Do something kind for your future self.

- Make a "love list" of things that make you feel alive.

- Ask: *"What would someone who loves themselves do next?"*

Relationships & Connection

I bring love into every interaction.

I attract relationships that nourish my soul.

I communicate with clarity and kindness.

My presence is a gift
to those around me.

— ◇ —

I see the divine in
others and in myself.

— ◇ —

I am safe to be
seen and loved.

I offer grace in all
my relationships.

⎯⎯◇⎯⎯

I forgive easily,
love freely, and
connect deeply.

⎯⎯◇⎯⎯

I am a magnet for
mutual respect
and joy.

I create space for
heartfelt connection.

My words uplift, and
my actions reflect love.

I trust the timing of
all my relationships.

I give from overflow,
not obligation.

I listen with love and
speak with sincerity.

***

I bring warmth
and welcome
wherever I go.

***

I release old wounds
and welcome
new harmony.

I choose connection
over control.

———◆———

I offer compassion
without conditions.

———◆———

I walk in love, always.

I attract people who
see me, know me,
and honor me.

———◆———

I welcome divine
relationships
into my life.

———◆———

I show up with
authenticity and
receive the same
in return.

I am surrounded by
love in visible and
invisible ways.

❖

I am part of something
greater—love moves
through us all.

❖

Every interaction is a
chance to spread light.

Good Day Practices for RELATIONSHIPS & CONNECTION

- Tell someone, *"I'm proud of you."*

- Leave a kind comment on someone's post—make it meaningful.

- Pray for someone who annoys you—then release them.

- Send a voice note instead of a text. Your voice has energy.

- Say thank you with extra feeling.

- Bless your home and everyone in it—*"May peace live here."*

- Call someone just to hear their laugh.

- Write a love note and hide it in your bag or coat for later.

- Hug a little longer than usual.

- Look someone in the eyes and really see them.

- Forgive someone silently. You don't have to carry it today.

- Smile at the next five people you pass.

- Say a kind thing to someone who isn't expecting it.

- Hold the door and send a silent blessing.

- Ask someone: *"What's been good in your world lately?"*

Creative Spark

I am a creative being,
made to express.

———◇———

I trust my ideas
and where they
want to lead me.

———◇———

Inspiration flows to
me and through me.

I make space for
my imagination.

❦

I create from joy,
not pressure.

❦

My creativity is a
form of prayer.

I allow my inner
child to play freely.

I am connected to
infinite creative
energy.

I honor the muse
by showing up.

I make beauty with
whatever I have.

❧——◆——❧

I am allowed to
make messy magic.

❧——◆——❧

I let ideas rise
without judgment.

I create what I need
to see in the world.

⸻◆⸻

My voice matters, and
my art is enough.

⸻◆⸻

Every small act of
creativity is sacred.

I flow with curiosity
and courage.

I make room for
lightness and surprise.

I breathe life into
the ordinary.

My soul comes alive
when I create.

I release perfection
and welcome play.

I am co-creating
with the divine.

I follow the spark
wherever it leads.

My creativity heals me and blesses others.

❦

I let delight be my compass.

❦

I was made to make things that move hearts.

Good Day Practices for
CREATIVE SPARK

- Doodle without judgment for five minutes.

- Play with crayons, markers, or paints like you're six.

- Write a haiku about your day so far.

- Make up a new name for yourself today.

- Try a different handwriting for your to-do list.

- Put on music and move like a tree, ocean, or flame.

- Describe your day in emojis only.

- Rearrange a corner of your space like it's a gallery.

- Write one line of a poem and tape it to your fridge.

- Create a mini vision board from magazine clippings.

- Sing to your coffee, tea, or smoothie. Yes, sing.

- Bake something just for the smell.

- Speak in affirmations all day—turn regular sentences into blessings.

- Draw hearts on your planner.

- Name the clouds and give them backstories.

Joy & Gratitude

I notice joy in the
little things.

—◇—

Gratitude is my
daily medicine.

—◇—

I am a witness
to beauty
everywhere I go.

I choose joy again
and again.

———◆———

I let delight
surprise me.

———◆———

I smile for no reason
and every reason.

I give thanks for who
I am and what I have.

❖

I open my arms
to wonder.

❖

Every breath is
a blessing.

I radiate joy and
reflect light.

———◆———

I find magic in
the mundane.

———◆———

I let gratitude be
my anchor.

I am surrounded by
miracles in motion.

❖

I give joy freely and
receive it fully.

❖

I celebrate life—my
own and others'.

I wake up grateful and
go to bed amazed.

———◆———

Joy is not a reward—
it's a right.

———◆———

I thank the day
before it begins.

My joy is contagious and needed.

❖

I find blessings where others miss them.

❖

I delight in being alive today.

I am grateful for
everything that
got me here.

———◆———

My heart holds more
good than I can count.

———◆———

I laugh, I praise,
I shine.
Gratitude is
my posture and
my prayer.

Good Day Practices for
JOY & GRATITUDE

- Write a thank you note to your past self.

- Celebrate something ordinary like it's extraordinary.

- List 10 things you love that cost $0.

- Pick a color and find five beautiful things in that shade.

- Keep a "delight diary" for the day— every little joy counts.

- Say thank you before every meal, even snacks.

- Make up a gratitude song and hum it.

- Notice something beautiful and whisper, *"More of this, please."*

- Laugh at yourself in the most loving way.

- Imagine joy as a glittery being walking beside you.

- Send out a wish for someone else's happiness.

- Thank your body for keeping you going.

- Notice one thing you normally take for granted.

- Compliment the weather—whatever it's doing.

- Dance like nobody's correcting you.

Purpose & Possibility

I walk in purpose
and power.

———◇———

I am aligned with
divine timing.

———◇———

I am becoming more
of who I already am.

I trust what's unfolding for me.

***

My dreams are not random—they are divine clues.

***

I say yes to what lights me up.

I move with clarity
and calm.

❦

My purpose is sacred
and evolving.

❦

I am ready to be seen
in my full expression.

I take inspired action with faith.

⸻ ◆ ⸻

I am the answer to someone's prayer today.

⸻ ◆ ⸻

I am equipped for everything that's mine to do.

I walk through open
doors with confidence.

———◆———

I carry vision in my
heart and courage
in my steps.

———◆———

I make room
for miracles and
movement.

I am willing to be led
and willing to lead.

I live on purpose,
not autopilot.

I choose alignment
over approval.

I am planted
on purpose, not
by accident.

———◆———

I give thanks for
the journey and
the destination.

———◆———

I show up as if it's
already working.

I trust what I feel
drawn to—it's
calling me forward.

⌐———◆———⌐

I am the creator of
my own becoming.
I let the divine
dream through me.

⌐———◆———⌐

I believe in what's
possible, even when
I can't see it yet.

Good Day Practices for
PURPOSE & POSSIBILITY

- Say: *"Something amazing could happen today."*

- Choose a word for your day and write it everywhere.

- Visualize one goal already achieved. Feel it in your bones.

- Take a small step toward something that matters.

- Say yes to an idea that excites and scares you.

- Write a mini mission statement for your day.

- Pretend you're your own mentor. Give yourself advice.

- Send out a pitch, proposal, or prayer.

- Ask: *"What does faith look like in action today?"*

- End the day by saying: *"I showed up. I am proud. Tomorrow, I rise again."*

GET YOUR FREE GIFT

Pick up affirmations, writing prompts and more at the official "Ask & It Is Written" website to start your day on a positive note!

Go to www.AskAndItIsWritten.com to get your free gift!

www.ingramcontent.com/pod-product-compliance
Lightning Source LLC
Chambersburg PA
CBHW070345130626
46556CB00007B/3032